TESTING THE SPIRITS

TESTING THE SPIRITS

by

Frederick K.C. Price, Ph.D.

FAITH ONE
PUBLISHING
LOS ANGELES, CALIFORNIA

Testing the Spirits
ISBN 1-883798-09-4
Copyright © 1995 by
Frederick K.C. Price, Ph.D.
P.O. Box 90000
Los Angeles, CA 90009

Published by Faith One Publishing
7901 South Vermont Avenue
Los Angeles, California 90044

Contents

Introduction

There are many people — Christians as well as non-Christians — who have a hunger for or a curiosity about the supernatural, mainly because they have not been taught what the Bible says about the supernatural. Rather, what they hear, in many cases, is that "the supernatural is not for us today." I even know of Believers who have heard or read about a so-called minister of the Gospel who, supposedly, had supernatural events happening in his church, so they went to see what was going on. What is happening most times in situations like this is that this so-called minister is not really preaching or teaching the Gospel of the Lord Jesus Christ, but some diverse doctrine. Instead of realizing this minister is not being used by God, but by Satan, the people allow themselves to be sucked into this person's "ministry," often with disastrous results.

At the opposite extreme are people who will be in a service where the Holy Spirit is moving — i.e., physical healings taking place, or the gift of divers kinds of tongues with the companion gift of the interpretation of tongues and the gift of prophecy in operation. But because they have never been taught that the Holy Spirit can and will move through God's yielded human vessels, they assume that what is happening around them is of the devil, solely because what is happening is supernatural.

Another variation of this theme is when people come into contact with a ministry in which "good" manifestations of the supernatural are taking place — people being healed of various diseases and afflictions, etc. The assumption is that since what is taking place is good, it must be of God.

Many people do not realize that not every supernatural occurrence that produces "good" or positive results is of God. They have not been taught how to know when something supernatural is of God or when it is of the devil. As a result, many people have been led away from the things of God by what they perceived to be the supernatural workings of God, when, in fact, it was a deception of the devil.

How can you know when something supernatural is of God, or when it is a trick of the devil?

This is what we will talk about in this book. We will look at what the Word says about the supernatural — when it is of God, and when it is of the devil. We will see how to prove it out with the Word when a supernatural event takes place and learn how not to be deceived when the enemy tries to pass off on us a counterfeit. The gifts of the Spirit — the supernatural moving of the Holy Spirit in the Body of Christ — are definitely for the children of God today. However, we have to know how to be ever vigilant in order not to be deceived by the enemy in his unending attempts to thwart the work of God in the earth realm.

1

Believe Not Every Spirit

1 John 4:1:

> Beloved, do not believe every spirit, but test the
> spirits, whether they are of God, because many false
> prophets have gone out into the world.

Behind every person who is supposedly ministering the Gospel, there is a spirit. We, as individuals, are
spirits, but we are also motivated or empowered by
spirits. When it comes to the things of God, it should be
the Spirit of the Living God empowering and impelling
us to do what we do. But we also have an enemy, Satan,
who is a master counterfeiter, and he will try to dupli-
cate whatever God does in an attempt to trick people
into accepting the counterfeit for the real. That is why
we are given instructions in the Bible to test or prove
the spirits. In other words, we are to check the spirits
out.

Notice what 1 John 4:1 does not say. It does not say
to test the prophets. It says, **...test the spirits....** That is
because a right or wrong spirit can motivate the
prophet, pastor, apostle, evangelist, or teacher, as well
as people individually.

Anyone who ministers the Gospel is supposed to be operating at the behest of the Spirit of God, but sometimes this is not so. This is because people have a right to choose to listen to whatever spirit they want to. If you are not careful and do not know how to test the spirits, you can be led astray by a malevolent spirit.

The Voice in the Tree

For example, there is the case of a very celebrated man whose name I will not mention. I am not trying to put this man down, but I simply want to use what happened to him as an illustration of how satanic spirits operate. In telling his story, this man said that as a young boy he had a very difficult time in school. He lived out in the country, and one day he was in the field near a grove of trees when he heard a strange noise in one of the trees.

He said he heard something like the rustling of leaves when a strong wind blows through them, but there was no wind. In fact, the air was deathly still. He listened for a while, then he approached the tree to see if someone had climbed up into it and was trying to frighten him.

When he got to the tree, there was no one there to be seen, but he heard a voice. He said the voice sounded so soft and sweet that he believed it to be the voice of an angel. The voice said, "You are having problems with your studies. I have come to help you. When you go home tonight, take all of your schoolbooks,

2

especially the one you are having problems with, and put them under your pillow, and go to sleep. I will do the rest."

That voice was a demon spirit trying to gain control of that person's mind. The person was just a country boy, so he did not know anything about such spirits. Even though his parents were religious in the sense that many people are "religious" but not necessarily godly, they were sincere people who meant to do right. Because this incident was supernatural, they assumed it was of God.

That night, the boy did just as the voice had instructed him to do. He put the book he was having trouble with under his pillow, and when he woke up the next morning, he knew everything in the book. From that time on, whenever this entity or voice would speak to him, he would know things without having previously learned them.

Eventually, it got to the point where he actually started working cures on people. What happened was that this spirit finally came inside of him. Demons are very subtle. They will make you think everything you are doing is all right because all the things you do under the demon's influence appear to be good.

What this man said he would do was to lie on a couch or bed and go into a trance. This entity would supposedly leave the man's body and go off somewhere — perhaps 50 or 100 miles away — to someone who was sick. This thing would supposedly go inside the sick person's body and diagnose what was wrong. It would come back inside the man, and the man would prescribe a cure when the sick person was led to contact him by the demon spirit. In every case, the cure was a combination of herbs and certain kinds of foods.

These cures were not supernatural healings by faith, but the people became well. The man's reputation grew until he became a well-known celebrity. People all over the country knew about him. They even created an institution named after him when he died. All of the people who were cured through this man thought the cures were of God.

God does not heal the way this man did. God's healing is by the Spirit of God — not by the foods we eat. Yes, we should eat right. We can open the door for Satan to have access to attack our bodies by eating wrong, and certainly some herbs are very good for people to eat. However, faith healing is not herb healing. God heals our bodies through our spirits by faith.

The supernatural cures performed by this man were amazing. He got my attention before I came into the knowledge of the Word. I did not know the things he did were caused by evil spirits and were very subtle ways the devil was using to draw people away from the things of God.

I don't know if this man was born again, because there was nothing ever said about the Lordship of Jesus Christ when these healings and so-called "miracles" took place. Jesus got an occasional mention, but that was all, *and Jesus being declared Lord of all is how to know what is taking place is of God.* If that man had known the Word, he would have known whether or not the voice was of God when he first heard it speaking to him.

4

Testing the Spirits

1 John 4:1-3:

Beloved, do not believe every spirit but test the spirits, whether they are of God; because many false prophets have gone out into the world.

By this you know the Spirit of God: Every spirit that confesses that Jesus Christ has come in the flesh is of God,

and every spirit that does not confess that Jesus Christ has come in the flesh is not of God....

1 Corinthians 12:1-3:

Now concerning spiritual gifts, brethren, I do not want you to be ignorant:

You know that you were Gentiles, carried away to these dumb idols, however you were led.

Therefore I make known to you that no one speaking by the Spirit of God calls Jesus accursed, and no one can say that Jesus is Lord except by the Holy Spirit.

These verses of scripture do not mean that a man cannot say "Jesus Christ came in the flesh," or "Jesus Christ did not come in the flesh." What these verses are saying is that a man cannot say Jesus came in the flesh and that He is Lord *except* by the Holy Spirit *if that man is supposedly ministering under the anointing.* When the supernatural appears to be in operation, but there is some question as to its legitimacy, that is when one can test the spirits. However, a person has to have the boldness of God to test the spirits in such instances.

The way to test the spirits is to say to the person through whom the supernatural appears to be operating, "In the name of Jesus, did Jesus Christ come in the flesh?" If the person is not of God and has an evil spirit, he will not admit it. If the evil spirit admits that Christ came in the flesh, he is admitting to his own destruction. Consequently, a demon spirit would not want to do that, because he wants to continue operating in and through the vessel he is using to do his dirty work.

Another way to test the spirits is by determining if all that the person says or does, while operating in the supernatural, is in line with the Word of God. In such situations, you cannot consider just one isolated phrase or word, but the person's total ministry and ministry style.

If there is a doubt as to which "spirit" is in operation, the person's actions should be followed very closely, and everything he says or does should be measured by the Word. If you know the Word, there is no way you can be deceived, and, thereby, you will be able to test the spirits.

If the Spirit of God is leading the person, what that person says or does will always be in line with the Word. He should be able to give thorough biblical evidence supporting his actions and not just an isolated scripture or event. He should be able to clearly show a pattern in the Word relative to the subject he is teaching or preaching on. Otherwise, without accurate biblical support, people can and have been led astray by a deceiving spirit.

Every Spirit?

In 1 John 4:2, John tells us that **...Every spirit that confesses that Jesus Christ has come in the flesh is of God.** Why does John say, "Every spirit"? After all, there is only one Holy Spirit.

The reason he says *every spirit* is because angels are spirits, as well as demons. Sometimes God will send angels to appear to people on earth. The Bible speaks of numerous occasions when these messengers from God were visibly seen by the saints of old. In fact, I have heard of people in our own day and time who have been visited by angelic creatures. However, no matter who comes or what is said or how wonderful or true the news might be, if that messenger does not acknowledge Jesus Christ as Savior and Lord, he is not of the Spirit of God.

Familiar Spirits

Because non-Believers, more often than not, know nothing about familiar spirits, they are often amazed when they attend a seance, supposedly to commune with the dead, and the transmedium tells them things that no one knew except the people who died and themselves. These people think they are actually in contact with the dead, and that they are experiencing the supernatural power of God. They do not realize there are such creatures in the spirit-realm called *familiar spirits*. These creatures are not of God, but they can know all about the people whom the medium is trying to contact and they tell the medium, through whom they manifest, what they know.

If God would permit you right now to see into the spirit world, you would see groups of spirit creatures moving all through that realm. In fact, these creatures are around us all the time, because the spirit world exists and operates concurrently with our physical world.

You may say, "I do not understand that." Well, think about your television set being able to pick up UHF and VHF waves at the same time, or your radio picking up FM and AM waves at the same time. In other words, you can flip the switch on your radio one way and you hear an FM station, or you can flip the switch the other way, and you will hear an AM station. All of these wave lengths are already in the earth's atmosphere, and there is plenty of room for different wave lengths to exist concurrently.

The spirit world works the same way, and we need to understand that. The important thing to remember is that there is nothing to be afraid of, because evil spirits have already been defeated. Jesus defeated them 2,000 years ago!

There are men and women around the world who call themselves "psychics" who give predictions to and about celebrities, as well as world events — such as who will win the Kentucky Derby. These so-called "psychics" do not realize they are actually being fed information by the devil. God does not care who wins the Kentucky Derby. A horse race has nothing to do with spiritual things.

Some of the things these people "predict" do actually come true. But it does not matter what they say or how often what they say comes true, the fact is that because something comes true does not prove it is of God. There are evil spirits who play games with people's minds and will cause things to come to pass just to keep them away from the things of God.

When God is involved, whatever it is will always have to do in some way, form, or fashion with redemption. That is why you can read the Bible from Genesis to Revelation, and it will lead you, sooner or later, to Christ. The Bible says in 2 Peter 3:9 that it is not God's will that anyone should perish, but that all should come to repentance. That is the first part of the Holy Spirit's assignment when it comes to dealing with the hearts of men — to help bring them into the family of God through their accepting Jesus.

2

Do Not Be Ignorant

1 Corinthians 12:1:
> **Now concerning spiritual gifts, brethren, I do not want you to be ignorant.**

This verse lets us know emphatically that God does not want us to be without spiritual knowledge. If you read this verse in the King James Bible, you will notice the word *gifts* is italicized. This means it was not in the original manuscript. This verse actually reads, **"Now concerning spirituals, brethren,"** or things that have to do with the spirit world.

If God does not want us ignorant about spiritual things, then we should not be ignorant. Unfortunately, most Christians *ARE* ignorant. They are ignorant because the churches they attend are ignorant, and the churches are ignorant because the pastors lack knowledge about the Word of God. For years, I was ignorant, and when the blind leads the blind, they both will end up in the trash compactor.

Counterfeits and Substitutes

There are all kinds of things the Bible tells us about, but which we very seldom hear a minister talking about from the pulpit. They are the things of God which the enemy counterfeits to draw us away from spiritual knowledge. The enemy throws these things our way to trick us into substituting them for the Word of God.

For example, there are churches which promote astrology, not knowing that astrology is satanic. I am not talking about the people who are reading or following after astrological signs, but the evil spirit behind this whole activity. There are satanic spirits that work through astrology to gain control of people.

Instead of searching the scriptures, some church leaders search the horoscope. *That is an abomination to God.* These leaders need to read what happened to people under the old covenant who were watching the sun and the stars looking for signs — *they were put to death.*

There is also what is called "soul travel." There are biblical references to this phenomenon. Soul travel is when someone lies on a couch or a bed and his or her soul supposedly travels to another country. When the person's soul supposedly returns, the person then tells some things about the place where his soul supposedly has been. When other people investigated what that person said about the country his soul visited, they found what the person said to be true.

"Soul travel" is nothing but a deception of Satan to catch people's attention. That person did not go anywhere. When he was in a trance state, a satanic spirit told him things and made him believe that he had actually experienced going to the place he thought he had traveled to.

Your soul cannot leave your spirit because your soul does not have a spirit. Your spirit has a soul, so it has to be your spirit doing something in order for your soul to be involved. There are cases where God has allowed people's spirits to leave their bodies without those people actually having died. The norm, however, is that when a person's spirit leave his or her body, that spirit goes either to heaven, if Jesus is his or her Lord, or hell, if Satan is.

Because this is so important, I want to again emphasize that **whenever something is of the Spirit of God,** *Jesus Christ will always be at the center of it.* Jesus is not mentioned in soul travel; neither is He mentioned in astrology, or in seances, or anything like that. Also, all the esoteric "truths" that people learn in things like soul travel and astrology cannot be of the Spirit of God because there is no way to track them.

God has left us a way to track spiritual truths. That means you cannot be deceived unless you want to be. Of course, if you do not go to a church that is teaching the uncompromising, full-counsel of God, then you might become deceived. But the truth of God's Word is available to any and all who will place themselves in a position to hear it, learn it, and receive it.

The Helper Who Guides Into All Truths

John 16:7:

"Nevertheless I tell you the truth. It is to your advantage that I go away; for if I do not go away, the Helper will not come to you; but if I depart, I will send Him to you."

Before we move on, let's look at a scripture that will tell us exactly who the Helper is. In John 14:26,

Jesus is speaking and He says: **"But the Helper, the Holy Spirit, whom the Father will send in My name...."** According to the Bible, then, the Helper is the Holy Spirit. Let us continue on with this study, starting at the eighth verse of John 16.

John 16:8-14:

"And when He has come, He will convict the world of sin, and of righteousness, and of judgment:

"of sin, because they do not believe in Me;

"of righteousness, because I go to My Father and you see Me no more;

"of judgment, because the ruler of this world is judged.

"I still have many things to say to you, but you cannot bear them now.

"However, when He, the Spirit of truth has come, He will guide you into all truth; for He will not speak on His own authority, but whatever He hears He will speak; and He will tell you things to come.

"He will glorify Me...."

That is how you can tell when the Spirit of God is operating in a church, or a building, through an apostle, prophet, evangelist, pastor, or teacher. You can tell when the Spirit of God is operating, as opposed to an evil spirit, because the Spirit of God will always exalt, magnify, and point the people to Jesus Christ.

If the minister or individual operating in the supernatural does not point the people to Jesus, I advise you to tip-toe out quickly, because you are on dangerous ground — even though what is being said may sound good, religious, or even spiritual. The bottom line is that, as a result of the supernatural operating in a service, you should be better acquainted with the Lord Jesus Christ. That is the Holy Spirit's job. If the spirit is an evil spirit, it will exalt the man he is operating through and make the man the focal point, rather than Jesus.

Any spirit that is influenced, inspired, prompted, and anointed by God will NEVER say anything that is inconsistent with God's Word, and the Word points to Jesus.

"You Have To Get *My* Teaching!"

Here is a classic illustration of what I mean. Again, I am not trying to vilify anyone. I only want to use this man as an illustration of what I mean about glorifying man rather than the Lord, so that you can get a better understanding of what God is talking about when He tells us in 1 John 4:1 to **"test the spirits"**.

Some years ago, there was a situation in which a number of people were led by an individual into the country of Guyana in South America. All who went with this man to this place ended up taking part in a mass suicide. The leader of these people was the Rev. Jim Jones. He was their pastor at a church in Los Angeles, California.

I had heard about him from some of my church members. They said great spiritual and supernatural things were going on in this man's ministry and I should go and "check it out." We had just started moving in the Holy Spirit at the church I was pastoring at the time, so anything that even smacked of the supernatural, in terms of moving in the things of God, got my interest. I wanted to learn everything I could about the supernatural operation of God in the Body of Christ.

The auditorium where they were holding the meeting was packed when we arrived. (A friend of mine accompanied me.) The congregation had been singing for some time, and the place was literally rocking. Suddenly, a lady in the front row jumped up and said, "Praise the Lord, praise the Lord. Thank you, Jesus. Thank you Jesus, thank you, Jesus!"

Jones was sitting on the platform, behind the pulpit, with his sunglasses on. He came to the pulpit, looked down at the lady, and in a stern voice said, "We will have none of that here! You have to get *my* teaching." When I heard him say this, I thought, "What? You mean you cannot praise the Lord? You cannot say, 'Thank you, Jesus' here?"

Later on, when Jones got into his message, he told the congregation, while holding a Bible in the air, "You do not need this book! You have to get *my* teaching." At this point, I nudged my friend and quietly said, "Let's go." We left that place quickly!

"...do not believe every spirit, but test the spirits." In order to test the spirits, you have to have something as a guide to test them by. In other words, you have to have something as a norm or a standard to compare the moving of the spirits to in order to make an evaluation as to which spirit is in operation.

THE WORD IS OUR STANDARD! If you remove the Bible, we have no standard, no way by which to measure supernatural happenings. Jim Jones told that group, "You do not need this Book (speaking about the Bible]! You have to get *my* teaching," and look what happened. His followers went with him, sold their houses, left everything to go to a foreign land, and ended up committing suicide. That could not have been the Spirit of God telling those people to do that; he could not have been following the Holy Spirit.

There is no way the Holy Spirit will ever say, "You do not need this Book." If you are a salesman for IBM, you are supposed to sell IBM computers, not your own brand. If you contracted to have mountain spring bottled water delivered to your home every week, there is no way you would expect the delivery man to bring you sewer water. You are paying for mountain spring water, and that is what the man representing the bottled water company is supposed to bring you. He is paid to give you what the company tells him to give you, and not what he wants to give you.

The Holy Spirit works the same way. He gives you only things that are based on the scriptures. There is no way He will tell you to throw the Book away, because everything God tells the Holy Spirit to give you is based upon what is written in God's Word.

God uses men to proclaim the Gospel, but you have to test or prove the spirits that are behind what men say. Is it the Spirit of God talking through a minister, or another spirit? The only way you will know is by the Word of God. Even when you cannot initially understand with your head everything someone is saying, the Holy Spirit will witness on the inside of you about whether or not what the individual is saying is right or wrong. The Word will act as the bridge for that revelation.

3

"You Have Overcome Them"

1 John 4:1-4:

Beloved, do not believe every spirit, but test the spirits, whether they are of God; because many false prophets have gone out into the world.

By this you know the Spirit of God: Every spirit that confesses that Jesus Christ has come in the flesh is of God,

and every spirit that does not confess that Jesus Christ has come in the flesh is not of God. And this is the spirit of the Antichrist, which you have heard was coming, and is now already in the world.

You are of God, little children, and have overcome them, because He who is in you is greater than he who is in the world.

Notice that verse four does not say, "...and *are* overcoming." It does not say, "...*shall* overcome one day in the future. It says, **...and have overcome them.** That is not present or future tense, but *past tense.* In other words, it is already done!

The way we overcome evil spirits is through Christ, because Christ's victory is our victory. Jesus was our representative, and everything He did in this earth realm, He did for us. He did not have to do it for Himself, because the devil was never His master. No

19

demon ever had authority over Jesus. No sickness ever lorded it over Him. He came to earth for the benefit of mankind and subjected Himself to the things He subjected Himself to, not because He needed deliverance, but because *we* did.

However, we have to appropriate His victory by faith and apply it to our lives, or we will not *personally* gain the benefits of what Jesus did in defeating Satan, demons, death, hell, and the grave. To appropriate the victory, we must do two things, because victory is not automatic.

#1: Appropriate Victory By Faith

God sees us through Jesus, and we need to see ourselves the same way. God never looks at us by ourselves, because we do not look too good alone. When God looks at us, He sees the qualities of Christ in us. He gives us credit for having those qualities, even though we do not have them by ourselves.

When 1 John 4:4 says, **You are of God, little children, and have overcome them,** it means God sees us as having overcome evil spirits through Christ. We still have to go out on a day-by-day basis into the world where these evil spirits are and take the victory. However, we do not go to find out who the champion is; we go *because* we are the champions. That is why James says in James 4:7: **...submit to God. Resist the devil and he will *flee* from you.** The word *flee* literally means "to run from in terror." Evil spirits will run from you if you know who you are in Christ.

If you want to be in on what God is doing, you have to work with Him based on His set of parameters. He says, **"You...have overcome them,"** even though you may not have dealt with any evil spirits or demons as far as you know. Why does God say that we have already overcome? Because that is how God operates. According to Romans 4:17, **God...calls those things which do not exist as though they did.** That is how faith operates. It is the calling of *those things which do not exist as though they did,* that causes them to manifest in our lives.

God says, **"You...have overcome them,"** because God has only one way of talking. God always talks as though the task was already accomplished. God never talks in the future, but in the present. That is why everything in the Bible relative to God is always present tense. It is always *now.* Jesus, when speaking about His spiritual self, always used "I am." For example, He said in John 14:6, **"I am the way, the truth, and the life."** He got that from His Father.

That is what we have to do — learn to talk like God talks, even though it may not make sense to us when we are doing it. We have to say and believe by faith, "I have overcome them through Jesus," and stand on that belief based on God's Word, and not by what we think or feel.

#2: Make Sure the "Greater One" Resides in You

The second part of appropriating the victory in our lives is stated in the condition God gives us in 1 John 4:4.

Forget about the commas and other punctuation marks and read the verse this way:

You are of God little children and have overcome them because....

Because implies that we have overcome them based on a condition, and that the condition is whatever is stated after *because*.

...He who is in you is greater than he who is in the world.

The Greater One or "He who is in you" is the Spirit of God. Jesus is in us, of course, because Colossians 1:27 says, **Christ in you, the hope of glory.** But the way He is in us is by the Holy Spirit. For those of us who have been filled with the Spirit, He is our power source.

The power of God is the ultimate weapon we can use in our spiritual warfare. I do not say that to water down the importance of faith, because in this warfare, you have to know how to operate by faith and know how to release its force, as well. However, if you have the faith and do not have anything to release by that faith, you still do not have anything. To "overcome them," we need to use the combination of faith and power — they work together.

In Acts 1:8, as Jesus was going back to heaven, He told the disciples, **"But you shall receive power when the Holy Spirit has come upon you."** This automatically implies that they were without that power before the Holy Spirit came upon them. That is why He has to come upon us also to give us that same power. Therefore, if you are not filled with the Holy Spirit, how are you going to overcome them who are in the world?

We must have the Greater One residing within us to make God's victory work on our behalf. It is not a question of being better than someone else because you are filled with the Holy Spirit. Rather, it is a case of being in a position of advantage when it comes to the spiritual warfare we all have to face in this life.

Reading With Denominational "Sunglasses"

There is one very important thing to keep in mind when it comes to studying the Word. When you read the Bible, do not read it as if it were a Baptist Bible, or a Lutheran Bible, or Methodist, Catholic, Presbyterian, or any other denomination.

What happens most times — particularly for those who have gone to one church or denomination all of their lives — even without their realizing it, is that people tend to read the Bible with their denominational beliefs in mind. They may not say, "This is my denomination's Bible," but they still read it colored by their denomination's doctrine. And just as everything seen through a pair of tinted sunglasses takes on whatever color the glasses are, so is the Bible often interpreted by those tied to their denominations. Consequently, when they come across certain scriptures, their minds automatically go blank. In fact, they may not even see some verses in the Bible because their denomination does not preach or teach that doctrine.

This is simply the tendency of human nature. I did it myself for many years without realizing what I was doing. It is a very subtle trick Satan uses to keep us from walking in the knowledge of the Word of God.

Here is an example of what I mean. If you have spent any time at all in a denominational church, do you recall anyone ever asking you while you were at that church, "Have you received the Holy Spirit since you became born again?" The chances are you were never asked this question.

After I became saved, the first church my wife and I joined was a Baptist church. The people in that denomination told me that being filled with the Holy Spirit was the same thing as getting saved, that being filled with the Spirit automatically happened at the same time I became born again. This is a commonly held belief, but it is a belief that is not scripturally correct. Let me prove it by the scriptures.

Acts 19:1-2:

> **And it happened, while Apollos was at Corinth, that Paul, having passed through the upper regions, came to Ephesus. And finding some disciples**
> **he said to them, "Did you receive the Holy Spirit when you believed?"**

Why would Paul ask a question like that if being filled with the Holy Spirit was something that automatically happened when you received Christ. Would Paul not have known that? When you are sensitive to the leading of the Spirit, you can tell when the Spirit is not operating in a church. Paul detected that something was missing that he did not consider normal.

Keep in mind that the events in Acts 19 took place approximately 19 years after the day of Pentecost. The Church had been operating in the power of the Spirit for all those 19 years. Paul at this time was about nine or 10 years into the full-Gospel ministry of the Lord Jesus Christ, so he definitely knew what he was doing by this time.

Acts 19:2-6:

> he said to them, "Did you receive the Holy Spirit when you believed?" So they said to him, "We have not so much as heard whether there is a Holy Spirit."
>
> And he said to them, "Into what then were you baptized?" So they said, "Into John's baptism."
>
> Then Paul said, "John indeed baptized with a baptism of repentance, saying to the people that they should believe on Him who would come after him, that is, on Christ Jesus."
>
> When they heard this, they were baptized in the name of the Lord Jesus.
>
> And when Paul had laid hands on them, the Holy Spirit came upon them, and they spoke with tongues and prophesied.

If what they told me in church were true — that you receive the Holy Spirit at the same time you become born again — why did Paul ask the people in Ephesus, **"Did you receive the Holy Spirit when you believed?"** His asking that question implies that being filled with the Spirit *is not* automatic. Also, Jesus says in John 14:17 that "the world" — meaning sinners — cannot receive the Holy Spirit. If you are filled with the Holy Spirit at the same moment you become born again, you are receiving the Holy Spirit while you are a sinner — and that is impossible, according to what Jesus said.

The Holy Spirit is a gift, just as salvation is a gift. To become born again, you have to make a volitional decision with your mind and your faith to accept the fact that Jesus is the Son of God, that He died for you, and that by accepting Him as Savior and Lord, you can be made a new creature in Christ Jesus.

Jesus says in John 3:16, **"For God so loved the world that He gave His only begotten Son, that whoever believes in Him should not perish but have everlasting life."** Salvation is not something that is automatically conferred upon anyone. It is a gift— but a gift that has to be wanted, asked for, and received.

Likewise, the Holy Spirit is also a gift. Acts 10:45 tells us, **...because the *gift* of the Holy Spirit had been poured out on the Gentiles also.** A gift is not forced upon anyone. You have to willingly receive it. Therefore, the Holy Spirit is in you only if you receive Him by an act of your will, *after* you have been born again. That may not be theological or traditional, but it is Bible.

God Says We Need the Holy Spirit

Acts 1:4,5,8:

And being assembled together with them [this is talking about Jesus, who was about to go back to heaven after His resurrection], **He commanded them**

not to depart from Jerusalem, but to wait for the
Promise of the Father, "which," He said, "you have
heard from Me;
　"for John truly baptized with water, but you
shall be baptized with the Holy Spirit not many days
from now...."
　"But you shall receive power when the Holy
Spirit has come upon you; and you shall be witnesses
to Me in Jerusalem, and in all Judea and Samaria, and
to the end of the earth."

Jesus *commanded* the apostles to wait at Jerusalem to
receive the Holy Spirit. He did not suggest; He did not
ask, and He did not inquire whether or not they could fit
it into their busy schedules. He commanded them to
wait for the promise of the Holy Spirit.

Notice the time frame when Jesus said the apostles
would be witnesses for Him: It was when they received
the Holy Ghost. Notice, too, that it was not until they
were filled that they had any boldness, ability, or
power. Before then, they were in the Upper Room cow-
ering, timid, and afraid. But when they were filled with
the Holy Spirit, these disciples and followers of Jesus
became bold as lions.

How can people today say they do not need the
Holy Spirit? Are they saying they are more spiritual
than Peter, James, and John? They have never seen
Jesus or experienced the miraculous in His presence.
These men saw Him, talked to Him, heard Him, fel-
lowshipped with Him, and walked with Him for three
and a half years — yet, He still told them they would
become witnesses **when** they received the Promise of
the Father. If we say we do not need the Holy Spirit, we

27

are calling God a fool, because God would not give us something we did not need.

I am not saying that Spirit-filled Christians are better than those Christians who are not filled with the Spirit. That would be like saying a baby born without legs is not alive. That is not true. The baby could be very much alive, but he would definitely be at a disadvantage because he will have problems being as mobile as babies are with legs.

I am not saying that Christians who are not filled with the Spirit are not born again. If you have accepted Christ as your personal Savior and Lord, your name is written in the Lamb's Book of Life, and you will go to heaven when you physically die. That is Bible. What I am saying, though, is that for anyone who is not Spirit-filled, they are at a disadvantage — the same disadvantage as a legless baby is, physically, in this world.

4

The Spirit of Truth, and the Spirit of Error

1 John 4:1-6:

Beloved, do not believe every spirit, but test the spirits, whether they are of God; because many false prophets have gone out into the world.

By this you know the Spirit of God: Every spirit that confesses that Jesus Christ has come in the flesh is of God,

and every spirit that does not confess that Jesus Christ has come in the flesh is not of God. And this is the spirit of the Antichrist, which you have heard was coming, and is now already in the world.

You are of God, little children, and have over-come them, because He who is in you is greater than he who is in the world.

They are of the world. Therefore they speak as of the world, and the world hears them.

We are of God. He who knows God hears us; he who is not of God does not hear us. By this we know the spirit of truth and the spirit of error.

Notice, in verse six, **...the spirit of truth and the spirit of error.** All truth, relative to knowledge of God, is caused by the Holy Spirit. And all error, relative to the knowledge of God, is caused by what can be called the "unholy spirit."

The Spirit of Fear

For instance, did you know that fear is a spirit? Second Timothy 1:7 informs us, **For God has not given us a spirit of fear, but of power and of love and of a sound mind.**

The Spirit "of power and of love and of a sound mind" is, of course, the Holy Spirit. If you let the Holy Spirit guide you, you will have a sound mind, and you will have power, because that is what Jesus said you will have. The love of God is shed abroad in our hearts when we are born again, and it is by the Spirit that we love.

Notice what is also said in that verse: **Fear is a spirit.**

There are some people who are afraid of dogs. If you fear a dog, that means the dog has a greater place in the world economy than you do and that an animal is greater than a person. That is illogical.

There are some people who have a fear of heights. Still more have a fear of enclosed places. Others are afraid of flying on airplanes, even though most of them have never flown on an airplane. Actually, these people are generally not afraid of the airplane itself, but of dying in an airplane crash. Satan uses the situations and circumstances of life to attack and dominate us.

Because of what these spirits have done to cause people to fear, people are afraid of all kinds of crazy things. When many of these people look logically at what they are afraid of, they realize it is stupid to have that fear, because really there is no sense to it. This is exactly the point. It is not sense — it is spiritual.

Fear — or Respect?

Many times, we use the word *fear* when it should not be used. In the majority of cases when we say *afraid*, we should use the word *respect* or *reverence* instead.

I respect and reverence fire, but I am not afraid of it. It warms the water and cooks the food in my house. It causes my car to have power so I can drive from one location to another. Therefore, I am not afraid of fire, but I respect it. I have a reverential fear of fire.

Reverential fear is the kind of fear the Bible talks about when it mentions the *fear of the Lord*. You do not play games with Almighty God. But you should not be afraid of Him to the point that you run and hide from Him.

We should reverence certain things. If a neighbor of mine has a sign on his fence that says, "Beware, vicious dog," I should not be scared of that dog simply because it is a dog, or move out of the neighborhood because a dog is there. However, I should have the good sense not to go into that yard where the dog is, because I have a reverential fear of vicious dogs.

Knowing the Spirit of Error

1 John 4:6:

...By this we know the spirit of truth and the spirit of error.

31

Every Christian ought to know the **spirit of error** and when he is manifesting himself. How are we to know? *By the Word!* That is one reason Satan has kept the Word of God out of the average church — kept it out in the sense of keeping individual people from getting a hold of what is really in the Word, what it is really for, and what it really says.

As I said earlier in this book, without the Word, we really would have no way to judge whether the Spirit of truth or the spirit of error was manifesting in our midst. We can become so engrossed in a matter that we can forget about the reality of that situation. We do that many times when we watch a movie. After a while, a person can become so wrapped up in the characters that he or she can actually feel sorry for the people on the screen — and the people on the screen are not even people dealing with real situations, but actors impersonating imaginary characters.

You cannot go simply by someone's performance when it comes to determining whether or not something is of God. Some ministers can put on an Academy-Award-winning performance and people can end up going to hell because they were so convinced by that performance.

You had better know the Word for yourself and be able to judge everything by God's Word. The "spirit of error" will work through the spoken word just like the Spirit of truth will — but he will twist the Word just far enough out of context to impart a false faith. Faith comes by hearing and hearing by the Word of God, but false faith also comes by hearing. That is why words — and **the** Word — are so important.

Being Observant — With the Help
of the Holy Spirit

What makes anything that is of the "spirit of error" so insidious is that it looks like the truth. That is what fools people. You probably have never seen a counterfeit three dollar bill, and probably never will, because there is no such thing as an authentic three dollar bill. The United States government does not print three dollar bills, so there is no reason to counterfeit them. You counterfeit only what is real.

Even if we are observant, sometimes it is easy to mistake the counterfeit for the real, simply because we are not perfect. I once worked as a cashier in a market, and one of the other cashiers took a counterfeit $10 bill from a customer because he was not paying too close attention. It looked like a real $10 bill. Even if you are observant, sometimes counterfeit money can look so much like the real thing that you have to have an extremely sharp eye or look at the bill through a magnifying glass to tell the difference.

By the same token, Satan will not come at you with some outlandish story. He will come at you with something so close to the truth that it can fool the average person. That person can be someone who goes to a church where they do not teach the Bible. However, it can also be someone who is taught at least part of the Word, but is not filled with the Holy Spirit. In other words, he may not have the Greater One living on the inside of him to give him signals as to what is right and what is wrong.

Knowing the "Spirit of Truth"

How do we know the **Spirit of truth**? By being filled with Him. That is how, because He will help us to be observant. By His leading and by the written Word of God, the Holy Spirit can help us decipher whether what is going on around us is, in fact, of the Spirit of truth or of the spirit of error. But if the Holy Spirit does not live in you, how will you be able to tell the Spirit of truth from the spirit of error when something is spiritually manifested?

Everyone in error is not a bad person. Many times these people have just been deceived and did not know they were being deceived. I was deceived for years relative to the Holy Spirit and did not know it. I assumed the people I listened to knew what they were talking about.

5

How to Be Filled With the Holy Spirit

After reading about the Spirit of truth and the spirit of error, you may have realized that you need the Holy Spirit to help you know when something is not of God or when it is. If this is the case, receive the Holy Spirit today — right now. Do not be led astray by anyone. Search the scriptures for the truth of God's Word. And the truth shall set you free (John 8:32).

Paul tells us in 2 Timothy 3:16-17:

> **All Scripture is given by inspiration of God, and is profitable for doctrine, for reproof, for correction, for instruction in righteousness,**
>
> **that the man of God may be complete, thoroughly equipped for every good work.**

Read God's Word with a heart ready to receive His revealed truth concerning being filled with the Holy Spirit and speaking with other tongues. Specifically, read the Book of Acts, as well as 1 Corinthians, Chapters 12, 13, and 14. I know the Lord will reveal Himself and His truth to you in this most important matter.

The following are some tips that will help you to receive the gift of the Holy Spirit when you are ready:

POINT ONE: The first point, which is absolutely essential as you prepare to receive the gift of the Holy Spirit, is that you must have accepted Jesus Christ as your personal Savior and Lord. John 7:38-39 informs us that the Promise of the Holy Spirit is made only to Believers. By no means should anyone who is not a Believer pray for the gift of the Holy Spirit. Here are some scriptures you may check to be sure of your salvation:

John 1:12	John 5:24	Ephesians 2:8-9
John 3:3, 5	John 6:47	Acts 16:31
John 3:16, 18, 36	John 20:31	

If you have checked these scriptures and say, "I do not know if that is me or not," or "No, I know that is not me. I have never received Jesus," here is how simple it is to be saved. Romans 10:9-10 says:

> **that if you confess with your mouth the Lord Jesus and believe in your heart that God has raised Him from the dead, you will be saved.**
> **For with the heart one believes unto righteousness, and with the mouth confession is made unto salvation.**

Do you believe that God raised Jesus Christ from the dead? Have you confessed Jesus as the Lord of your life? If you have not confessed Him, and would like to, pray the following prayer aloud:

"Dear God, You said in Romans 10:9-10 that, If I confess with my mouth the Lord Jesus and believe in my heart that God raised Him from the dead, I will be saved.

"I believe that Jesus Christ is your Son, and that He was sent into the world to redeem my life. I believe that He died for me, and that He was raised from the dead for my justification. Jesus, be the Lord over my life. I confess You now as my Savior and Lord, and I do believe it with my heart. According to Your Word, I have now become the righteousness of God in Christ, and I am now saved. Thank You, Jesus. Amen."

Romans 10:13 says:

> For "whoever calls on the name of the Lord shall be saved."

You have called upon the name of the Lord, so salvation is yours now. The scriptures listed under *POINT ONE* now apply to you. Confess them as yours, believe and receive.

POINT TWO: After you have read the Book of Acts and 1 Corinthians, Chapters 12-14, let the Word show you that the Holy Spirit is meant for every Believer today. Read the following passages of scripture carefully.

Joel 2:28-29	Mark 1:8	Luke 11:9-13
Matthew 3:11	John 1:33	Luke 24:49
Luke 3:16	Mark 16:17	

God says that in the last days He will pour out His Spirit upon all flesh. There is no expiration date or statute of limitation. All who seek the Holy Spirit may find Him.

POINT THREE: Remember that the gift of the Holy Spirit is not given as an attainment or reward, based on some supposed degree of holiness, but based alone on the fact that Jesus promised to give Him to every Believer, freely and by grace. Below are some scriptures you may want to check:

John 7:38-39   John 14:25-26   John 16:12-14
John 14:16-17   John 15:16   John 16:7

POINT FOUR: When receiving the gift of the Holy Spirit, it helps to be with a group of Spirit-filled Christians who can instruct, encourage and pray with you. Although it is not essential, I personally find it to be a great help for two specific reasons.

First, because it is scriptural. Acts 8:17, 9:17, and 19:6 show us how others may help us by the laying on of hands as a point of faith release.

Second, because Satan will immediately challenge the Believer as to the authenticity of his experience, it is good to have the witness of Christians who can affirm the authenticity of the experience.

POINT FIVE: Now that you are ready to receive, simply pray this prayer of invitation:

"Father, I believe with all my heart, based on the Scriptures, that the gift of the Holy Spirit is meant for me. Just as I have trusted You for my eternal salvation by faith, so now do I trust You, by faith, to give me the

fullness of the Holy Spirit with the evidence of speaking with other tongues. I now receive, by faith, the gift of the Holy Spirit. Thank You in Jesus' Name, Amen."

POINT SIX: Release the Spirit by praising the Lord in tongues (it will be a language you will not understand) by faith, as the Spirit gives the utterance or language. Remember, the Holy Spirit does not do the speaking, *YOU DO!* This is what happened to the disciples on the day of Pentecost. Why would the Lord deal any differently with you? He is no respecter of persons or denominations.

By faith, open your mouth and yield your tongue to the Holy Spirit. Trust Him to give you a language of praise. Initiate syllables with your tongue and lips. Remember, that even when you speak in your own familiar language, unless you open your mouth, give the sound of your voice, and move your tongue and lips, nothing comes out. Often unfamiliar words will flash into your mind. Speak them out in praise to the Lord. The more yielded and believing you become, the more fluent and free your language will become.

If at first your language does not "flow," do not become discouraged or doubt that you received the gift of the Holy Spirit. The devil may suggest to you that you are making it all up, but do not listen to him. Remember, the devil is a liar and the father of lies. Continue stepping out in faith by yielding your voice to the Lord.

POINT SEVEN: Continue to exercise your gift daily. Like an athlete preparing for competition, you must "stay in shape" by giving your new experience a daily workout. Keep praying and singing in the spirit. If at all possible, seek other Spirit-filled Christians to associate with. And above all, find yourself a Spirit-filled church that is teaching the uncompromising, full-counsel of God. That is the way to grow and stay ahead of the devil.

It is important — if you want to be a victorious, overcoming Believer — to not only be filled with the Spirit and be in a Spirit-filled church, but also you have to study the Word of God daily on your own. That way, the Spirit of God can educate you through the Word of God on the will of God and how He and the "spirit of error manifest" themselves around you. I cannot emphasize it strongly enough: **YOU NEED THE WORD *AND* THE HOLY SPIRIT.** Being filled with the Spirit is not the end of all spiritual revelation. It is only the beginning.

When you allow the Holy Spirit to lead and teach you, you will not only gain revelation knowledge, but you will have the potential of becoming a powerful and effective witness for Jesus Christ. For this reason, plus all the others I have mentioned in this book, the devil will try to intimidate you, and try to rob you of God's best. *Do not let him do that!*

Keep your eyes on Jesus, the author and finisher of your faith; hold fast to the Word of God, which abides forever, and soon you will be firmly rooted and grounded in this new life in the Spirit. The Word of God says you can overcome every obstacle through Christ Jesus, because the Greater One lives on the inside of you. Let that sink into your spirit, let the Holy Spirit guide you so that you can grow in God's Word, and let Him help you live the overcoming Christian life as powerfully as God says you can.

For a complete list of books and tapes by
Dr. Frederick K.C. Price, or to receive his publication,
Ever Increasing Faith Messenger, write

Dr. Fred Price
Crenshaw Christian Center
P.O. Box 90000
Los Angeles CA 90009

(continued on next page)

BOOKS BY FREDERICK K.C. PRICE, PH.D.
(continued)

THE WAY, THE WALK,
AND THE WARFARE OF THE BELIEVER
(A Verse-by-Verse Study on the Book of Ephesians)

BEWARE! THE LIES OF SATAN

TESTING THE SPIRITS

THE CHASTENING OF THE LORD

IDENTIFIED WITH CHRIST:
A Complete Cycle From Defeat to Victory

Available from your local bookstore

About the Author

Frederick K. C. Price, Ph.D., founded Crenshaw Christian Center in Los Angeles, California, in 1973, with a congregation of some 300 people. Today, the church's membership numbers well over 14,000 members of various racial backgrounds.

Crenshaw Christian Center, home of the renowned 10,146-seat FaithDome, has a staff of more than 200 employees. Included on its 30-acre grounds are a Ministry Training Institute, the Frederick K.C. Price III elementary, junior, and senior high schools, as well as the FKCP III Child Care Center.

The *Ever Increasing Faith* television and radio broadcasts are outreaches of Crenshaw Christian Center. The television program is viewed on more than 100 stations throughout the United States and overseas. The radio program airs on over 40 stations across the country.

Dr. Price travels extensively, teaching on the Word of Faith simply and understandably in the power of the Holy Spirit. He is the author of several books on faith and divine healing.

In 1990, Dr. Price founded the Fellowship of Inner-City Word of Faith Ministries (FICWFM) for the purpose of fostering and spreading the faith message among independent ministries located in the urban, metropolitan areas of the United States.